Absolute Pleasure

Katrina Marie Johnson

Order this book online at www.trafford.com
or email orders@trafford.com

Most Trafford titles are also available at major online book retailers.

Note for Librarians: A cataloguing record for this book is available from Library
and Archives Canada at www.collectionscanada.ca/amicus/index-e.html

Printed in Victoria, BC, Canada.

ISBN: 978-1-4269-1972-5 (sc)

ISBN: 978-1-4269-1973-2 (dj)

Library of Congress Control Number: 2009938919

*Our mission is to efficiently provide the world's finest, most comprehensive book publishing
service, enabling every author to experience success. To find out how to publish your book, your
way, and have it available worldwide, visit us online at www.trafford.com*

Trafford rev. 12/2/2009

 www.trafford.com

North America & international
toll-free: 1 888 232 4444 (USA & Canada)
phone: 250 383 6864 ♦ fax: 812 355 4082

"Dreams are illustrations, from the book your soul is writing about you."

Marsha Norman

To mi Amore, poiché ti amo
And to Kristina Emmerson
For giving me the courage to live.

A Forward

As Irving Layton sang his love of women in low tenor, I sing my love of men in high soprano. He envisioned a body, lustful and quaking, young and diligent; I envision a body, aged by time, experienced, patient, and strong. Cleopatra, Madam de Pompadour, Josephine Bonaparte, and Roxelana all saw fit to praise the prominent men they loved. So do I. As heartbreaking as love may be, and as often as it occurs, we should never turn our heads away nor let our hearts decay.

The first love of my life was no doubt the oldest man I knew. He was bright eyed, charming, and most of all, irresistible in words. He spoke of romance, lips, cherries, and above all compassion for the mystery of women. I knew certainly in the pages of D.H Lawrence that I had found love in its purest form. His written words kissed me slightly in the neck, until my soul could feel nothing else. I felt the rhythm, I felt the emotion, and finally I felt the passion of poetry. Although my childhood coo over Lawrence was innocent and inspiring, Layton was a full blown love affair, if not a sexual one. Not only was my soul groped by a genius, it gave me the key to my ultimate freedom. I began to eat, breathe, and live the philosophy of love. Free, sensuous, lustful, immoral, even frightening passion was everything I desired, needed and wanted.

Each individual artist bases a small extent of their work on a particular flavor. My own taste for this collection of poetry is that of female passion and its consequences. Within the unrealistic world we live in, the expectations and the bonds of morality leave the female sex to strive for more than that which should be allotted. Still to some degree, a Victorian idea of morality still remains, and if anything, suppresses a woman from fully exploring her sexuality. In my own opinion, women should not fear the opinion of others, instead fear the opinion she has of her own conclusions. No matter what situation we may be in, no matter with whom we may fall in love with, take your found happiness by the horns and hold true to yourself. If we do not take chances, we could end up spending most of our time regretting rather than reminiscing on the naughty or sinful things we could have done. A lady must deviate from a common path, and take the road less traveled in order to find sure happiness.

Viva Mi Revolutione Di L'Amore

The Artist Is Born

What spark, what villainy is this!
To achieve the informadable
To lie down with the devil
The creation of artifice.
In this I mingle with him
Having loved and lost everything,
Achieved and gained nothing.
I lie beside him breathless,
Loving not and living whole.

I died inside,
With nothing but an edge
Of what the poet once was,
Beside his fifty-nine years
And nineteen of mine.

The person moralistic and true
With not a word to contribute,
The artist is born through heartbreak

And adultery.

Dreams of the First

A day before my lover shows
I dream of you alone
In a bed with me,
Whispering your many faults
Fighting with my many evils
You've killed me.
Thoughts of moving on,
Constantly wither away
When you're in my head.
Four months have passed,
Yet memory still haunts.
The dreaming must end.
Even though you'll not see me
Or hear of my name,
Your always in my heart,
Even when I'm with
The one I hold in the highest.
A father and teacher,
Kissing his aging skin
And feeling his warmth behind me
I think of you.
When he grabs me in passion,
Forming exotic Kodak's
And suppressing my desires
I see you.

Who Am I?

My name is irrelevant.
I am a person.
More importantly a person
With feeling.
I am your dragon.
I am humble, yet powerful, persuading.
Those who do not follow me
Drown in the depths of pathetic sorrow.

Not only an artist, a poet and priest,
I am whatever you want me to be.

Nothing can stop me.
It is nothing of which I am born of
Or die from.

You fear me, yet you still return.
I can either love or hate you.

Don't you know me?

We share the most kindred of friendships.

Who am I?

Blind

The heart is,
The heart was,
A pantomime of flow.

Beseeching,
Endearing,
And deathly,

It barters on poisonous grip.
Having crushed,
Having opened,
The lost world awaits.

Aspirations lie,
Cantering raw personification.

We lose ourselves
And live our chance
Having looked,

But didn't see.

Unfeeling

I never know what to think
When you push my embrace away.
After the act of lust
You lie there entirely,
After I did all the work.
You resisted my honey charms.

What to do with you?

Next time we're as one
And your asleep,
I'll creep out the door
Past your white guardian
And leave you to insanity.
Perhaps then, when dawn rises
And your alarm buzzes,
You'll feel as used

As I do when I'm with you.

Buried Hearts

My only love has mine beating heart,
Locked away as it were.
Under stones, sand, clay and earth.
Beating steadily in its crafted box
It bleeds and aches for him always.
No vessel or life line attached,
It lives on through his memory.
The way his love fed mine
Could wake the dead from eternal rest.
As he held it in his silky hands
It grew in size and leaked within.
With his touch my heart bleeds.
A life force needs the other half,
To live on, and live life as intended.
It bled and ached so often I asked,
If he could make our love one.
There and then he pressed his lips
To my very soul, swallowing my heart.
Blood running down his chin
This way, love and future in present form
We were one as fate would have it.
Wherever he went, so did I.
Now mine love is cold and grey.
The heart still beats within its box,
Under sand, stone, clay and earth
I forever remain cold.

The Boss Man

Swindling silence he keeps divine
Secrets he keeps from those in time
Lusting after ladies so fair
Breaking hearts without a care
Picking lovers in a reach
Crossing lines he should not breach
Sleeping with a broken part
Mending with a bleeding heart
Guards her close with eager eyes
Lacking truth to his demise
Dwindling sight in bitter age
Coupled with a yearning rage
Swelling in his ancient loins
For one he buys with colored coins.

Birth of a Realization

Urging. Wanting. Feeling
Lips on lips
Power on fear
Passionate exchanges
Both for lust
One for the emotion
The reality
The other for a spoon
Cream filled start.
Wrinkled sheets
Thrusting domination
As life spreads the world
Continents apart
Sliding earth's core
To the center womb
Overthrowing man
The reign is over.
Shrinking under light
He shouts his faults
Crowning her glory
The woman has arrived.*

Ovarian Trip

Over.
It's over.
I've wakened from this toxic dream
How forsaken it has been.
All reality drugged away
Shielded by a rubber snake
Its teeth, locked to my works
And protected
By natures sappy linen
That binds us all
To a subdued kind of grace.
Addicted,
Yet not forgotten.
As the tide washes away,
The footprints still remain
Between prison and life,
Self confessed,
Of the pleasure brought,
But all the same
Miserable, desperate
Lonely without a place *
And a sapling to harvest.

Excuse of an Abandoned Bride

I live in self torment
Enjoying the chase of sin
But the proper lady inside
Was cruelly murdered
By vanity within.

Lost Hope

Grand master, what a fool are you!
Taking on a lover so young,
Thinking she's the only one
Who truly understands the man
With all her twenty years,
When all her woman see's
Is the boy who killed her hopes.

Linguini

Flopping from side to side
Grey as a corpse
Wrinkled as a prune
Barely convulsing
Dead to the senses
Lifeless to sliding touch
"Please darling think of me." I say,
"I can only try." He responded,
Wiping down, disappointed,
I cry in frustration.
"You're finished." Said I,
"How do you know?" Said he,
Throwing his penis to the wall
It stuck in place
Turning back, I said,
"Your noodles are cooked."
Turning away,
He cried.

Societies Abortion

A rainy day at long last,
Admitted. Screamed. Confessed,
Reborn, my arm straight.
Reading into the world
To sequins, drug, poverty,
Mind altering gum and paste.
I surrender and give
My body, soul, all there is.
Bohemian lore and life
Cradles the babe I am.
When wholly dejected from,
Artless state reality
I sup on bottled imagination,
Conceived in the very womb
Of societal rejection.
Confirming creative Holocaust
We remain as one, squirming pile.
Like worms surfaced by the flood,
Taking our greatest gift
Holding strong to the quill
Our clipped feather of freedom
Grasping only cold handles
That keeps our pens from dulling.
The stench of dripping caviar
Making blue of solid teeth
Lining every cracked smile
Defining deep cavity holes
We lie in decrepit earthly tones
Whispering emotions deep.
Locked away in heart strung vaults
We are the life, we are
Altogether, societies abortion.

Heartbroken Transition

Locked absolution, withered rings
The copper rusting
Disintegrating to green nothings.
A wandering look
For you darling, love another.
I see revealing lies
Tainted with guiltless demise.
My soul falling from the heavens
Weeping, I am dying.
Longing for the man you were
Veiling weak, dreary words
All forgotten in time.
I cease living. Breathing. Working.
Betrayal I cannot undo.
A twisting trail of hatred
Blocks the mind, confusion
Now I see your sex, your person.
Admit the whole a lie.
Trust, admiration, and jealousy
I tell your half farewell,
As you lie together in waste.
Business or pleasure Boy?
I've only time for one.

A Ghost

Give me a sign,
Distant ghost of mine.
How your eyes,
Melt away at the point of break
When daylight hits,
It melts away your being
And blinds your soul
From seeing.
Confess it all,
My dearest entity.
Tell the world you exist
Instead of howling
Into the mist.
For surely you will lose yourself
As you know not already,
You have been dead ten years long
And jaded to the notion
That I have struggled,
Fought through life in vain
Without a fleshy hand to hold.
Instead, you weep without a care
And I cry without a soul
For you are no longer there.

Guard Your Soul

The succubus dines on those who miss,
Scarred and trapped in its deathly kiss,
Flail and scurry in demonizing fright,
They do what's best to put things right.
Smelling, tasting, sticky red glue
Wandering at night;

They come for you!

One of Each

How can the addiction be slaughtered
When all is said and done?
With one love leaving,
Another one is sent.
So kind gentlemen are.
How playful and thoughtful.
However all for not.
They are a wasted source,
And how can I refuse either?
When both are sweet and kind?
Offering my only vice;
Compliments, gifts, and passion
How selfish am I?
When I use the beauty born
To bring these sub wealthy men
To a state where they care no more.
A life they've spent so hard to build
Risked at costly expense,
When fallen for the elderly
Your in their pockets hence.
But the very question lies,
Though I love my darling brown eyes
How is it to manage two
Without one seeing the other?
Or having relations few?
Both from European stock,
And charming on their own
But as Queen Elizabeth said,
"Why not marry one of each?"
When suitors have much to teach.

Beating Rhythm

Hold me darling hold me
Keep me near your beating heart
So that I may keep in time
Our rhythms far apart.

Often not I hear your soul
What little chance I get
But when the chance arises
I often long forget.

What Little Time

Long yet fast
The very way of life.
What little time we have.
All of us naïve,
Unsparing, unsaving,
Negligent of love.
What little time we have.

The hate harbored
And moments unconquered.
What little time we have.
When all is said and done,
Reflecting not on words,
Telling one another lies.
What little time we have.

All of us die,
One embracing the other.
What little time we have.
Please put all war aside.
Keep your darlings close.
Never question the person.
Oh what little time we have!

The Kiss

Lips parted fresh from fire,
Touch each other in pure desire.
Her delicate rosebud mouth,
Decided to travel South,
As he laid warm and gentle,
Upon a bed of flowers,
Counting only the hours,
Till his lover went mental.

Master Dear

Oh Master dear,
Where are you hiding?
When your mistress sits crying
Of unpicked fruit on her luscious vine?

How long it's been
Since your heavy touch
And smoldering kisses on,
The creamy skin
She keeps hot for you.

Sing to her your dreams,
Both low tenor yours
And high soprano hers,
Of simple delicate moves
In the clouds of the bedroom.

Longing for your tongue,
The weight of your soul
Pressing her to pattern
In those striped sheets
She calls her sanctuary.

Where is your touch now?
When it is needed most?
To pour water on the fire
That has run wild
Between your hips when one.

Naked curves remain behind
The peacock fan of lust,
As feathers open and close,
Revealing supple breasts
From which you always dine.

In the garden she waits
Praying only for release.
Come out from hiding dear sir
And whisper to your darling,
How belle and naughty she is!

The taste of your pleasant mouth,
The lingering Stetson perfume,
Drives her insane with desire
When she is hit with the whip
You flick so admirably.

Come and taste the fruit she bears,
Dine on the cherries you took,
From her garden most plentiful
And kiss the very red lips
That has your business on hold.

September Seventh Too Eighth

What a night promising master!
Bending to take the wrath,
Of the Mistress Coy
Whom you thoroughly enjoy.
Tasting the very snap,
Of her Russian Lord
On your aging behind
And yet you call her name
"Oh Tigress! Darling girl.
If I were twenty years younger,
We would make a life together."
She knows you silly fool!
With every strike she conquers.
Bending reality into dreams,
From sunset to sunrise.
Yet, when awake from heavenly state,
Finding her divine spirit
Asleep and unjudging,
The musky scent of her night-like hair,
Swells your masterly spirit.
Leaving the smoldering sheets,
To cleanse the heart for a new day,
You think of her hot skin
And her soft lips upon your chest.
Upon your return to her,
There is only dying embers,
The outline of where she lay,
The earrings she bore,
And your blood on the pillowcase.

The Greatest Perfume of All

Shelves stalked high with colored viles,
Hundreds to see for many miles,
Only one can hold the key,
To my lustful memory.
A musky scent laced with spice,
An ocean breeze and something nice,
A dab of sweat au natural,
Ingredients I swear, all factual
A dash of coffee succulent,
Stir it well and let ferment,
Squirt a gram of potent Axe,
Add a stick of sealing wax,
Throw a cup of Chardonnay,
All these things would make my day!
Dip a strand of colored wool,
Drop of oak and stir in full.

The Death of Virginia Woolf

Slowly gazing upon the roof,
Stands alone Virginia Woolf.
Walking along the fields abroad,
Thinking of whispers, silly sod.

Feet resting on flattened grass,
Sadness comes so chilling and fast.
Hands around the heavy rock,
Put in the pocket of her battered frock.

Stepping in cold and thrashing waters,
Thinking nothing, nothing matters.
Feeling the rush of icy cold,
Slowly returning to maker and mould.

Lungs are filled with Jackie's knives,
How long she lived with tainted lives.
Two days goes by as river flows,
The fate she made is one she chose.

Without word the writer appears
On the river bank, born from tears.
Her skin pale, mouth of water,
Once held delight and peachy laughter.

Now at peace, she cries no more.
Silent now like never before.
Eyes fixed on pale blue sky,
Her subtle way saying goodbye.

The Art of Seduction

How does one seduct?
Tis as simple as day.
Look at your lover
As if you were fatherless,
A lone girl in pain.
Pout as if disappointed
And purse your lips,
As if you were mute.
Catch him in his lies.
Be always a head,
Five steps to be sure.
Give in to pleasure
With all your soul.
Release the caged temptress
And leave room for mystery.
Act as if royalty,
A gem in your eye.
Know your beautiful,
Nothing more sublime.
Be ever 'faithful',
Never let secret slide,
And take him by surprise!

Sunrise

Pretend you have no feeling
Sweet. To be content
In the world of craftsmen,
The settlement weak,
On hallowed grounds
Burrowed to the last,
Leave the darker days
Long and far behind.

Sleeping Beauty's Truth

I, the flawless beauty
Put to sleep
Like a dog in heat,
Rattled my coma chains.
For if the witch,
Had any brains,
She'd have forsaken
Her darlings Kraken,
And left me to
My weary games.

Birth of a Child

Flakes of Stardust spill down to earth,
Giving life through to birth.

Sweeping down to vision of fame,
A lovely being I've given a name.

Walter

Hey Mr. Matthau!
Dead long before I'd grown
I'd come to love you,
Watching your Oscar best,
Wishing I'd have known you.
My penchant for older men.
How my belly moves,
When I hit the rewind
Because I like you that much.
It's all too bad
I wasn't born
Forty years ago.

Writers Block

Tis a humorous thing,
How thoughts come and go
Through points of production,
At times on a low.

One moment I'm scribbling,
The next dribbling,
In one path fertile,
The other dry and brittle.

No movement of plot,
Forsakes the right of hand,
To sit and think not,
Turns the brain to sand.

Is This Love?

My heart is fluttering,
My body restless.

I can't stop thinking
Of he who cares.

He may be old,
He may be troubled,
But he is mine.

In spirit,
Body
And soul.

When I see his person,
I tell him I like him,

Because I'm too scared,
To tell him I love him.

Victor

To the very core of it all
Strewn up in life's cobwebs
You dance with exhilaration
All because your life has purpose
A meaning to someone whole.

My Big Bust

I must

MUST

Go bust

BUST

From your lust

LUST

Because of just

JUST

Mistrust

TRUST.

Unchained Slave

A livelihood
Tied in red laced satin,
Puckered lips
Painted
In sapphire rouge.
Black webs strewn,
Along her widow legs,
Bound, pinned
With pink bow fangs.
A familiar near,
Laying at her feet.
Emerald glow
Of eyes watchful.
Dark
As if nightfall.
No one is to cross
The path of darkness.
A slave she is
And never a master.

The Great and Small

Within the explicit
Red, raw
Adulterous rigorous flaw,
I wonder on high,
Why I even
Need it at all.
Through caged darkness
And coined forsaken eyes,
Passed by and by,
In all self absorption
There is leaking,
By the great and small,
The adulterous, rigorous flaw.

With resemblance to the beholder
And business to cling to,
I weep with dissolution
Asking myself the question,
If all is cut to shape
To all an ideal plane
Why do I need it,
Even at all?

Remains of the evening,
Cold and harsh,
Yet hot in my hands,
Leaves upon the dawn,
Abandoned on the form,
Of a blissful caress,
A quick kiss in stride
As though a sweetheart
I left hand to confide.

And there the line breaks,
The birds begin a song,
Of debutants retreating,
Plush layered petticoats
Removed and stained,
Strung through the wash.

Spotted sheets shielded
Not a drop of blood spilled
The adulterous, rigorous flaw.

I'd Die For Love

Dancing in the shadows,
I long to hear your voice.
Stepping on the gallows,
To clearly show my choice.

Kiss me softly sweet lover,
How I envy your praise,
Your presence is a hover,
From my youthful, dreamers daze.

Home After A Weeks Bliss

Tu donne un bouteille vin,
Dans un sac de chien,
Wishing teary farewells,
To darling Satan hell.
Regard ton coeur est vert,
Come le froid Atlantique mer.
Never letting her in
Despite that lustful chin.
Dit et pencerais le future
Avec elle, au couture.
Since you erase all hope,
Let alone, cut the rope,
Regard ce beaute rare,
Maintenant regard quesque tu fais.
Your castle coming down
For the little girls gown,
Est rouge avec tes sang
Quand tes penis est dans,
Her soul morality,
Keeper insanity,
A ca chambre de torture,
Et guarderais la future.

The Concern of an Old Man

Content I am to be rolled,
Tied up in this plain of disaster,
Or to have my back stabbed,
My knees broken, or teeth ripped out.
Do with me what you will,
But never while I'm alive
Will you take my cherub away.
Small and big in name
Her cups hold more than water.

Transitioned Poet

Leave it to the devil and fool
A tarot plastered
It's remnants on the table
I look up from the reading
Into vain and struggling eyes
He is surely a daemon.
A brown and supple guise
Draining and hypnotized
I am weak
All becoming of release
Drowning in agony
And swimming in sorrow
Penetrated by the force
Of that vivid succubus
Who bleeds me dry.

He has stolen my skin.

Shimmering Piscean scales
Stapled onto Scorpios shell
He consumes my insides
And fills my fingers anew

I let him steal my soul
All because I was netted
By a fisherman in love.

La Routtura

The Madam

On behalf of those below,
I can never admit defeat,
To say I was never so,
Would be an evil cheat.

From innocence was I bred,
To a life bitter and dry,
Forced into a filthy bed,
With a boy I did defy.

A union broken, god bless,
It saved my soul from rot,
Not settling for any less,
Brittle tears long forgot.

Loving only those who pay,
Keeping the madams silence,
Whom I serve I cannot say,
It only ends in violence....

The Cat

Lurking around the center of the city
Cat of all cats sneering around the corner
She doesn't know it
But she's changing in so many ways
Fighting, aching, crying
She smells the others near
Driving and scraping her claws into the ground
She stretches, insane delight
No one will ever catch her
No one will ever keep her
No one will always love her
She's the Cat of all cats
With stinging eyes and broad grin
Cheshire laugh, she backs into the shadows
Without reason or cause
Cleaning her long silky tale
She waits for her prey to come to her
Napping and foraging daily
She survives well, best as she can
No children or life
She silently suffers without affection
As her long lashes curl
Her hair beating against the wind
She is the Cat of all cats
Men taking her for granted
She harvests a mark on every victim
Claws that could cut flesh from bone
She is the Cat of all cats.

In Dreams

I live alone.
Alone in a room of wonder with
Poetry freshly plastered,
Taped along the walls.
Assured, yet plucked from place
Once a new thought begins.

I rape, am raped,
And glue the pieces
Together.
The book, easy to read.
Written by far too many.

I utter speech through the mouth,
The voice that doesn't sound.
Parched for thirst
With touch of my spine,
I die
And am reborn.
Guilty, made guilty.
Innocent, born free.

Not a number,
A live woman
On hand,
In high demand,
Sitting atop a world
Without a god to preach.

Insane Dreams

Sleep deprivation is almost romantic.
Spirits sulking, taking in a soul,
I watch him sleep away the sanity.
Dead brown eyes wander under their lids,
The world moves depressingly slower,
Dreams are filled with fear of time
With little comfort swelling the mind.
I try to fall the same way,
Billowing to the land of faeries,
So that I may wander softly
In the shallow waters of the black sea.
Ridding a motorcycle without crashing,
Or skinning my knees.
I'm flying through the air
With my arms spread wide,
Swimming in the waters
Breathing in without drowning,
A fish in the sea,
A bird in the sky,
I'm a chameleon,
Always looking for new colors to try.
In dreams,
There's endless possibilities.
Sleep has been disturbed.
My vacation interrupted,
Time and time again.
Melted canvases and crusty paint,
Old and stale are all.
Good times are never remembered,
Neither are the bad.
Whatever happens in Wonderland,
Stays curled and floating,
Secret with Lewis Carroll,
Without memory to live with.
Thankfully madness is contained,

A tinder box laced opium,
But which is really sane?
Worth living for?
Worth dying for?
Only my dreams can lead me to insanity.
Once you find a place,
Your very own reality,
Content only exists
When you find a spot to lie.

The Blood Countess

Going about the usual play,
She saw a blemish on the day,
Her skin looked pale, her eyes a flutter,
Cutting through her maid like butter,
Rubbing the secret in her arm,
Killing off her lucky charm,
Keeping silent of victims many,
Trading lives for youthful penny,
Holding faith and revolting age,
She kept her ladies in a cage,
Bathing daily in blood galore,
She heard the serfs come through the door,
They tied her up and held her down,
And came across her spattered gown,
With fear they ran out to the yard,
And found the nearest palace guard,
Asking him for explanation,
He pointed out a sad location,
With desperate hands they shoveled dirt,
Revealing hair and battered skirt,
Pulling daughters from shallow graves,
Removed they were, in tidal waves,
The Countess found herself in bind,
For her crimes and twisted mind.

Drunken Wake

Shimmering Consciousness,
I awake to the night.
Having indulged faithfully,
In lovers pure delight.

Drunk to all the senses,
I found him gone and ran,
A blow to caring thus,
Wishing he'd been a man.

Robert Dudley's Lady

Existing amongst fields of thorns,
She waits in her prison, mourns.
Fearing those she leads astray,
Waiting for him, one of clay.
Hardening and softening,
She moulds him in her hands,
Taking his love, casting it,
To the center of her sit,
Between her thighs, she cries fast
Without a mould to cast.
Forever royal, in stale thoughts,
With only lust ever sought.
Longing the moments in the sun
Over love she could not have won.
For the other woman stands,
Locked in a cage of withered hands
That meant nothing to his mind,
In their secret meetings, timed.
She flew with the seasons,
He stayed and had his reasons.
In this the sovereign lived,
On the hill the court forbid.

The Weaker

The guilted vision
A tiny smirk
Lot confusion
From little jerk.
His boyish gaze
The slight of suit
In tempered rage
Prolonged pursuit.
Killing easy
No love in turn
Ladies queasy
Sitting concern.
Growing lonely
He's lost in hate
Sadly homely
In poor estate.

Lovers Lament

I'm out
I'm gone
Without a face.
A laugh
A bribe
In Shameless grace.
I fall
I stand
On broken feet.
I smile
I cry
In all defeat.
With all
Without
A strong heartbeat.
I live
I die
Until we meet.

Cleopatra's Rant

You call upon me, yet do not flinch,
Claim you love me on every inch,
But do you see my soul of old?
A Queen of Egypt, or so I'm told,
Lavishly dressed in trains of silk,
Sulking around my bath of milk,
I was a God to my unknown,
So why do I feel so madly alone?

The Royal Asylum

Knock, knock, knock,
The lights are out.
Knock, knock, knock,
Silent desperate shout.
Knock, knock, knock,
Clinically off.
Knock, knock, knock,
The clock has stopped.

Horizontal Lifeline

A tragedy, a cry
An accepted fate
One half
Finds its other
A lifetime of searching
Only
Forty years to late
One married
One varied
Both sparing
Of minutes
Hours
Days.

No More

Three months long I have waited.
All too patiently for praise,
God knowing, your lawyer hands
Have ceased to keep me caring.
Firing off letters to keep your busy mind alive,
So adequately go ill responded.
All that is lost,
Your lady of the night,
Who dwells on lust, touch, and gore
Sleeping pride away at length,
I cannot love you.
I will not love you.
Let all decree my final choice,
Written in the book of shadows
To be uttered. Murmured upon ceremony.
I give up, for my heart longs no one,
No how and nothing.
Save for the riches life can bring.
Though at once my mind caged
With the sanctity of binding,
He to my heart who had failing.
Fighting long with a foaming tiger,
You plucked me from the war
With all intentions sacred.
Only proving yourself a jailor.
Damnable lawman you are,
Stead of a radical running bird.
The bars are open as they always were,
Through the free and violent domain.
I will take my chances.

For Roger

Longing painful loss
I cry alone.
For every man I see
Reminds me of you.
The innocence and pain.
The hurt and charming.
All in the eyes of the man
Whose brown reflection I hold.
Not dead but cast away,
Recovering self anew.
I can't tell you how much
I need and miss you.

Lady Down

Plans to hold her cavalry,
Pulls her down eternally,
The lovely lady strong and true,
Fell as fast as Xanadu,
Once beheld a rosy air,
Sits alone in royal chair,
Brushing out her velvet flow,
Tying hose with ribbon bow,
Passing long in prison room,
Waiting long for monarch doom,
Careless trust lost in day,
Locked by husband on display.

The Emotion Is Gone

What is this feeling?
An endless pit of joy?
Or a cage of misery?

Thoughts of passion?
With Mister coy?
That all can see?

Or is it love?
That blinds me so?
With tales of passion?
Tales of woe?

Oh dreaded thing!
Keep away!
For moral decay
Sets in with ring.

I cut you out eternally
To this game of life
Ending the strife
Rest my soul to be.

Hit The Curb

I smite you down old friend,
From a path you couldn't mend,
All in all I won the war,
Your forgot an oath you swore,
For you are nothing to me,
Never are and never were,
After all you couldn't see,
The evil and vindictive her.
The very core of me.

Search for Mother Earth

Weak and drained,
I know it to be true,
For much is falling,
In a manmade paradise.
How pleasant we try to be,
This dark, weary world.
Fearing the angered mother,
We keep our legs in, curled

And how we roam this earth,
Searching for the very cure
That turns us all to dust
From the land we procure.

Mankind

Resting with the first and only,
Dreams at the door to reality,
Remains locked and stone cold.

After having the heart broken,
When child rests inside
And father denying his claim,

She loses herself entirely.

I lose my faith in mankind.

Its Over

Lover dear, I can't go on,
When I have waited weeks long,
To feel your wriggling beneath,
My sitting upon your sheath,
Our affair has come to end,
You cannot put out to send,
Me into my wildest dreams!

University Hunt

Trembling hands and shuttering voice,
Unsure thoughts show his choice,
History clear on boards he writes,
Itself alone in tainted lights,
Brown shoes and purple shirt,
Slips of chalk you must insert,
That tie! That wonderful thing!
I'd love to pull it close to bring
A kiss, a nudge, a sudden cry,
The poor professor, so very shy!

Loyal Succubus

You made me what I am now,
Reminisce at your fine work,
Stand up straight and take a bow,
Instead of being a jerk.

Take me now you filthy bastard,
Teasing me the way you do,
In the best you have mastered,
Torturing the Kitten too.

Shut your closest pride today,
And ravish the youthful girl,
Quit the evil games you play,
That make your day-dreams swirl.

Find I can be forgiving,
To the only human man,
Into sickly upbringing,
I can have over again.

Without care and commitment,
I am truly a rosy winner,
To get your loyal shipment,
Of dedicated swimmers.

If Lola Were Here

Demand of him everything
Right from the very beginning,
To least know where you stand
In his ancient foreign land.

The Monster That Has Me

So enchanting a man,
Keeps me running again,
From which I desire,
A crisp and bitter fire,
With none to hold me down,
In leaves I coyly drown,
Attempts to walk away,
Stop in fast on the day,
He laid me down coldly,
And spread my legs boldly,
Thrusting his aging spear,
Into history clear,
With no sense of caring,
In passion worth sharing,
He keeps the chains heavy,
Bound to charming steady,
Screaming for all to hear,
The monster keeps me near.

Daddy Mine

The way you treat us,

Just sit,
And say you'll leave the family.
The disease that runs through,

Has destroyed
What's left of you.

My Father Dear.

Guide The Girl

Wrapped warmly in the arms of a father,
Rests the parentless woman.

Selling herself,
For guidance only.

Hoping to become a daughter,
Loved and never forgotten,
Between thirty-three folds,
Of painful separation.

Self Cleaning Oven

A kept and locked secret.
The chest of hopes and dreams,
That once beheld an expert lock,
Now frail and gone with use.
Not old nor rusting,
Wise nor perfect,
But failed in all purpose.
A box to hold the future
Jumps loose on every seal.

Obsession

Hopeless
A victim of passion
I cannot see
A simple factor of being
But the face,

The face that haunts
My dreams to being.

I see,
I see but only her.

Black hair,
And sharp brown eyes.

A willing.
My willing.

Anything is hers,

Whether it be diamonds,
The knowledge she yearns,
In books,
The pages crisping.
The experience longing.
I give to her,
And her but only her.

Lost Touch

We all see signs and numbers.
1,2,8,17,33,19,52...33, 16, 33,
All in a row,
They glow deeply in the letters,
Far as I know.
Those visions are so very dear.
I cannot go, nor blink with fear.
They be gone,
Sudden chill,
Crash the car,
To sudden thrill.
Seeing things not even there,
They locked me up,
It isn't fair.
I'm a genius, so it be,
To live in state reality.

Back To Slutshire

As the courtiers gather close,
The King puts on his crown,
Kissing away his mistress,
In dismal, missing frown.

How fair and beautiful,
The girl who won his heart,
Knowing he could do nothing,
But relate his love in part.

Taking his face in her hands,
She whispers her farewells,
Speaking of their next meeting,
Under hope and wishing wells.

Four trumpets sound,
The Queen is home from Bath,
A King waiting in silence,
From his lustful aftermath.

Walking down the court,
She sees the Duchess serf,
Shivering in the presence,
Of her rising, plumping girth.

Frowning in dissolution,
She faces her pleasant other,
Waiting for an answer,
Of this young, expectant mother.

Sitting upon his thrown,
The King looks to the night,
As his wife sits beside him,
Despite all their marital fight.

Taking hands they join in part,
As the Duchess returns to shire,
The ruler crying inside,
Of the child he did sire.

6:45 pm

In twenty-four hours,
I will be twenty years old,
Living with all the powers,
Of the restless, young and old.

Through the history down,
I read over my actions,
Slowly removing my crown,
Screaming chapters are fractions.

The Final Meeting

When Caesar comes to do his bidding,
Cleopatra will not take part in sitting,
Away she sails along the coast,
From the man she wanted most,
Alone with ease she cries no more,
Acting Queen, but not a whore.

Dinning with the Elderly

Last night I lay in bed,
Uncertain what to think.
Curled up on the other side,
The old man rolls over,
Stroking my arm,
Entangling our thighs,
He sighs with jealousy.
My youth is invaluable.
As his tainted secrets are open,
Silence plagues our night.
He whispers softly,
I cannot answer.
Shocked.
Disgusted.
Surprisingly emotionless.
Sinking from his lies,
My body stiff,
"You wouldn't have loved me otherwise."
Lids come to close,
Hoping all had been a dream.
The sun rises.
I am torn apart.
What to call him now?
Despite no relation,
Boyfriend?
Lover?
Father?
Grandfather?
Friend?
I'm crying inside.
But play the game anyways,
Because I know it all too well.
In this moment,
We find ourselves alone
Dining apologetically.

He says nothing
While I take apart
Every wrinkle on his face.
Hunger suppresses anger
And the menus are laid to rest.
He smiles.
A tongue is swallowed.
Blood is tasted.
The heart pumps faster.
I stare into his aging eyes
And see his glasses on the side,
"Go and get your education."
Betrayal, understanding,
I find my voice again.
No longer suppressed,
I smile too.
"Thanks Dad."

Drifted from a Kindred Spirit

My chest caved when I saw you.
Mollusks a plenty,
Lining themselves to the starboard side,
And without a tool to scrape the sea,
I was at a loss,
Bobbing alone with fright.
The wind,
No longer filling my sails
As the eyes of my babe
Are set to drift.
I threw a bottle to wander,
And when read,
Told of the love we shared.

No one realized,
Or truly envisioned,
The lie, all a fairytale.
A simple fabrication,
Of a delusioned woman
Lost at sea.

Alone

Tyrannies faults.
Broken implements of torture.
A rusting cage.
Empty halls.
Fountain pens dry.
The writer ceases writing.
I am lost.

Living On

Inside my heart is breaking,
Despite all I'd been faking,
The falsity, makeup and powder,
The show only grew louder,
I'm a hero no more,
Only a lousy, sick whore,
Painting what men desire,
Having been thrown to the fire,
When the art looses worth,
And lies plump to girth,
I teeter on the wake,
And dance for my own sake,
Breaking many hearts in gore,
Careless when shit hits the door,
I will live on as always,
Though breathing through a haze,
Of dark misconceptions,
I live with all intentions,
Something they don't understand,
When they spit and condescend,
I'm getting on, living thus,
Through filth and manmade puss.

Burn the Vacant Self of One's Own Making

Look at yourself dear lover,
And recant the people who were once at your bidding.
Your eyes, plush with admirable affection,
Now lost aimlessly with age.

You've grown dull papoose.
Not enough to hold the eye of one so great,
Like a rancid goat you wander,
Carrying with it no thought of distinction.
Lost to the world in search of sustenance,
And taking in the scent of the decrepit afterlife,
Which you fear to be sacrificed.

Go lover go,
While there is still time and place,
Leave the poet to esteem her raging thoughts,
Soaked in sin and putrid upbringing,
Leave her to the mare,
So she can suckle every last ounce.

For you have no milk to give.
You have nothing to share.
Save for the eyes to the world you have wandered,
Most commonly alone.
Lost to all that is human.
Lost to all that had remained.

All has turned sour.
Your teats are no longer brazen,
No longer full and holding.

You are dead,
And you HAVE lived

For the babe, cradled this year long,
Has grown to state of decay.
The old goat
Has been led astray,
From the power,
Of the haunted suckled fowl.

Nothing At All

All in a little twig
Does the density
Of freedom wake lie,
Cut down in fields
On a vast summers day,
Looming solo in the wind.
Having been cut and dried
So that I may forget
How many days I've tried,
Once the fire is lit
And the ash holds the flame,
I'm on the way to salvation.
Startling gorging puffs,
I reawake with vigor,
Feeling nothing at all
And drinking in the flavor,
Of a skunky, juicy mix,
Not erasing the truth,
But holding it.
Floating above the gloomy day,
Till the very sun comes down.

Get Down

Leave me to this accord
For I cannot afford
You to stand
This tall
When I am
So small.

See Minus

In the time you took
To raise and pass,
All should have been left
Undone and yielded,
Shielded to the better man.
Instead the years dragged on,
Sinfully undescribed,
Envisioned alive,
And through the intestines lie,
A crumpled nurse,
Ill as can be,
The philosopher,
Bitter and cheated,
The poet,
Who sheds a daily tear.
One rushed to the band
Barely living on strength,
The other one fatherless,
A man of his own inner hell.
The last pursuing,
Delusioned,
From a fatherless home.

This is what you have created.

Answerable

Move in passing
From every faithful.
The rays from heaven
Enraptures your soul to speak.
AN ANSWER
Is expected,
Demanded,
From the idol you have praised.

La Regina Et Coronata

An Ode Too Our First Year

In The midst of all that is
Dark,
We have fashioned one another,
For you my darling,
Are my greatest poem.

I have died
Many times over,
In the heat of sensation,
For your creation.

Do I regret
Or will ever
Forget?
Never.

For I, am the ultimate
And you,
Are my equal.

My lover, my master, my dear.

A Life Away From Life

Let us go home Grand Master,
Home to hot, sandy lands,
Without humidity,
As I hate the heavy air,
And you need a breeze,
Because you are growing old.

Let us travel by litter,
Over and along,
The grand, flowing Nile,
Like the Cleopatra and Caesar,
That we once were.

Enjoying the sounds of the sitar,
Plucking away our heartstrings,
Eating plums and curry,
As we float away from life.

Together, holding each other,
As the Giza and Sphinx go by,
Feeling the warmth,
Of our bodies as one.

Oh the cold Egyptian nights!

Let us explore the ancient tombs,
Singing the histories of old,
And like drunken Anthony,
Renounce your contract
And make me the Queen I am.

Let us forget our troubles,
And bathe in milk and roses.
Fingering the gold bracelet,
Which keeps this Queen

Forever tied to the Kingdom.

Dine with slaves at our feet,
Sharing a golden cup,
Dressing us with sacred oils,
A landmark in our name,
A final resting place,

Where we can be together.

A morning sun, tanning our skin.
Ra, blinding us in his midst.
Blessing our sinful union,
And elevating us for eternity.

Let us be immortalized,
And forever stay at home,
Abandon our decaying existence,
In the very country,
Of changing seasons.

A place where we will live,
Day after day being reborn,
Renewing our lustful passion,
Where we will be preserved,
Our names chiseled,
On sacred temple walls.

Let us go down as King and Queen.
Our life away from life.

An Immortal Beloved

Like Beethoven I panic,
Not knowing,
Whether to let you in,
Or shut you out.
Not knowing,
Whether to live,
Or die,
Without you.

With every sip,
Of brazen Merlot,
I think of you,
Immortal beloved.

To go on
Mercilessly,
Knowing your here
And plotting your coarse
Not knowing,
Where we'll go,
Or what we'll do.

Not knowing,
Where we'll meet,
Or where we'll end.

But this I do,
To the very core
Love you.

Chain me up,
In paramour wreck.
For I know,
Eternally long,
That I indeed
Love you.

I Refuse

I refuse to follow the blueprint.
I refuse to be dead.
I refuse to read newsprint.
I refuse a dirty bed.
I refuse to give up my lover.
I refuse the courters sighs.
I refuse my own mother.
I refuse to tolerate lies.
I refuse the weary touch.
I refuse second place.
I refuse fucking much.
I refuse a desperate face.

National Treasure

Sweet perfect stance,
An ideal setting,
The timeless moment,
In heavenly bedding,
Rest forever joined,
Caged for none to handle.
Two of the finest grapes,
A jewel in the sun,
Robust, and earthly,
Encouraging, and shy,
White resting with red,
Chardonnay on Merlot.
Dusty filmy sheets,
The signature of time,
A taste beyond measure,
Split seconds lived,
The glossy spring,
Tinted yellow pear,
Oak lined mine,
Releasing the senses,
The sun has risen,
A fresh years start,
Aged to taste,
In a sixty year bed,
Next to forever young,
The dreamer of cold,
The autumn winter,
Purple swirl cabernet.
A mix of all that is old,
The remembrance,
Of historic lust,
Icy, shriveled berries,
Mixed in bloody wars,
Symmetrical key holder,
The old in mind,

Created past twenty,
Sits awaiting the day,
For the right mouth,
To taste their loyal chastity.

Life In The Big City

The calling of the ghetto streets,
Rosenthal off Caldwell,
Five gunshot blasts.
I lie awake,
Unstartled, unaffected,
Calm and collected.
Cooing, sighing, expelling.
Safe upon my cloud,
Nothing else matters,
But the night who lay asleep,
Draped in gossamer sheets.
Rolling to my vanity,
Assuming me veiled,
Parted from this world,
With all visions unfurled.
He lay his hands upon me,
Caressing every curve,
Powder hazed mystic,
Taken in defeat.
In his grasp the moon,
Cupped in his feeble hands,
Moving down the universe,
Swallowing the stars,
Near and afar.
The woman is alive,
For he can only strive,
Vicariously breathing,
Like a child's teething,
Through the soft milky way,
He becomes the morning dew.
The early dove calls,
Filling passion walls,
The cloud has fallen,
Grounded to the shore,
Regretting even more,

The call of the day,
Watching him turn away,
Shedding from the light,
I claim my warrior,
My rugged gentlemen,
Dead set masculine.
I'm only female,
Searching for a husband,
Who will make me a legend
Despite my livings.
The big city round,
From the crust I found,
He is not the one,
My life has only begun.

Forest Floor

Romantic fits of passion
Come and go in intervals of three.
Through two realms I cannot see you,
Blinded by rays not of this world.
My life is black and white.
In this I fear to move.
Crawling on hands and knees,
I feel it all without you.
Nothing but forest floor,
Wet and crisp in my palms,
In everything I hear you.
Robbed without a name, a face.
My knees long worn to bone.
Sticky blood marked my travel,
The length gone, seeming eternal.
When truly faring inches, not miles,
It is clear I have failed.
Being loved by you is subjection,
A willing imprisonment,
A thriving fertile life-force,
Like a breast ready to suckle.
Our story spurs creativity,
Floating through time and space.
When one, nothing matters,
But the clock forever strikes,
The union ever failing
And my strength wearing thin.
Bits of earth cake the wounds,
Yet alone I remain unscathed.
I sink in a single bed,
Filled with flowers, twigs, insects,
Letting the circle reclaim me.
Hiding every part you loved.
No longer the lost daughter,
A babe in bid of attention,

But an eternal female of lore,
A woman in need of progression.

Dream at Twenty

A picturesque lovely setting,
How can anyone tell me
I cannot dream?
A flower bouquet,
Pickled with roses,
Sweet smelling, divine,
Laced with lilies,
All from the valley.
White in color,
Elegant in composure,
Wrapped in a bouquet.
How can anyone tell me,
I cannot dream?
A long white dress,
Tres Romanesque,
With glowing jewels,
Bound to neck and arms,
And a triton crown,
Gold bands of plenty,
All dreamt at twenty,
How can anyone tell me,
I cannot dream?

The Fate of Team M and M

Rolling around in pious grace,
Observing the sins of the flesh,
Belittling her every chance he gets,
Ever wondering what she truly is,
Reaching out far and wide,
Tracing her every step.

Insinuating the falsity of words,
Love can only go so far,
And in the end you wonder why,
Hate clouds begin to drown the sky,
You have failed yet again.

If all comes to a deep surrender,
You dazzle her with splendor wealth,
Hurt the shell that remains intact,
Meekly returning to your dragons den,
Inwardly regretting your decision,
Willingly you spur to run away,
Begging the girl once more for care,
Realizing how sore and lost you are,
Earning nothing from emotional return,
Awkwardly stepping aside, jealous,
Knowing you could have had her forever,
You have failed for the last time.

Standing Pattern

The pattern followed
Religiously,
Eloquently,
Decisively,
Each morning the Madam rises,
Wide to the morning haze,
Once lost in every shadow,
Reborn and glorified,
All to the summer air.
The light once stunning,
Slashing at sight,
Now warm and flowing,
To pleasant delight.
She stands tall again.

All We Have

Longing to be bound to you,
My sweetheart, lover, darling.
For none could steal away your space,
That has wedged a place in my heart.
Besides for suitors, there is none but you.
A simple peck by those lips means the world,
Though with passion lacking I fall,
Forever daring all morality,
Casting out what is both bold and coy,
I sit on a throne of untold daring,
And wait for the coming of your presence,
Knowing fully I have a path to lead,
Makes it all impossible for us,
Coupled, and yet never married.
For you are already dead inside.
Though a glimmer of hope I have seen
Floating away in your big brown eyes,
Is the truth behind your actions.
Deviants and rascals we are,
So dark and evil, yet innocent and blind.
I adore and love you good man of mine.
Hold me to your soul and I'd gladly drown,
For no other soul mirrors as well as ours.
So dance with me fair aging beauty,
Through the rest of your lingering days
And I will never prove you false,
Only coating you with longing.
For our love could never die,
What all we have,
You and I.

Back To Being a Mistress

All too many variances
Of sexual encounters,
Does this mistress dare.
But one chest of hair,
Holds her to sing,
An unbridled fling,
With he, unchasted fair.
Bringing truthful care,
Over the railing,
And into bed,
Kisses smoldering in law,
Entwines with what she saw,
On his naked being,
In love of conceiving,
Her passionate lusts,
In one she trusts,
To the extent of her heart,
In regions a la carte,
Golden thighs wrapped around,
His soldier, safe and sound,
Proclaiming his passions start,
With her legs spread wide apart,
Singing aloud his name,
On her stomach when he came.

A Whisper from the Master

The curl of her hair
Twisted around my finger,
The place of her chair,
Echoes in the halls.
They linger.

A Madam's Questioning of Long Term Commitment

Another visit,
Another rise,
Another day,
In long disguise.
How many times
Must I hide?
From the sacrament
Of conjugal tide?

I lie,
I'll die,
Here in this state
Of question why.

Imprisoned,
And chained,
Commissioned and pained

I see no reason,
Or point
In your blessing,
Your begging
To anoint.

To The Wife

Fall, fall, fall,
Dear lady tall,
For there is no compassion,
In your work, or fashion,
No matter how hard the action,
Or wide the pickled few.

I long for your place,
But detest it all the same,
For I will not fall under,
A false and hardened name.

Much do you have now,
A son to call your own,
For I could never carry,
A child on my own.

But nevertheless,
Single or childless,
I'll support your woes,
As your husband goes!

To The Husband

Be, be, be,
Dear slut I see.
Without the will to live,
You drag the chains abroad,
With only etches in the dust,
Soon to be blown away.

What little impact you have.
Taking what is sacred,
And hiding it from all,
Keep all for one,
And one for fall.

With all trust established,
Waiting for solitude,
An escape from destruction,
In your bowl of construction.

Autumn Waltz

The autumn leaves dance
Gracefully in tune,
Having once been young
And full of life.
Crisp away in the dark,
Waltzing their very last,
Upon the wind,
And across the veil,
Of man and whale.

November 24th 2008: My Thoughts In The Midst of the Lamplight and Falling Snow

As the snow falls
I find myself being held.
The light of the street lamps
Outlining our features
Through the open window.
I am at peace knowing,
In a few short days
We can lay out the mornings
And pretend in haste,
There is no reality.

A Lovers Ode

Oh powerful, dependable dear,
What I'd give to keep you near,
To taste and hear your fatherly praise,
Leaves me alight in oceans daze,
Cries abroad in angels sight,
Heard the call and killed my fright,
Held me close despite our age,
And freed your bird from guilted rage.

A Thought on a False Farewell

I see it in your eyes,
The painful break,
Whether it be
Your groin, or heart.
Whenever I say
Goodbye
My intimate friend,
Do you think
We should last forever?
When nothing in the end
Ties me to you.

Childs Eyes

Innocent are the youth.
I see it every day.
Couped in their learning minds,
Ever excited,
On lively finds.
Their big, longing eyes,
Drink the pleasures of the world,
Not knowing the dangers,
Of obscenities unfurled.
How frail they are in body,
And fresh they are in time,
A passion for a present growth,
When one of them is mine.

Little Gentleman

Little one I love you,
Coming home you never fail,
Scripting the words of my soul,
You know me above all,
Caring, not wanting.
Yearning for my embrace,
We have each other amidst the dark,
Recalling not your birth,
But born from pen and ink.
My signature on crisping papers,
All will die but we,
You are a man, small and frail.
Leaving behind your stench,
And the mess I must endure.
Dependent on every dime I earn,
But I'll never complain, no.
That lowly shelter
Delivered you into my arms.
All I need is you.
My sweet little gentleman.

A Pound Here And There

When the time for love is gone
I lose all sight of hunger,
Having no lack of nourishment,
I refuse it all together.
Nothing longer keeps me
Because I feel and want to feel,
But lack the cause for care,
And become an empty frame,
All because your absent.

Absolvable

We cannot be condemned fair adulterer,
For we are not the only ones
Who parade and flaunt ourselves,
Around the circus room.

You think I'd give up my reputation
All for your sake alone?
Well think again my darling,
I'm only with you for the show.

All your children have died,
Those harem ladies have gone,
We're the last products of darkness,
And think me your eternal whore,
I will fade away like all the rest,
Leaving you to burn alive at dawn.

I will not be condemned fair adulterer,
For I am not the married one,
You think I'd surrender life and love,
All for your sad tale of long.
Well think again my sweet,
I won't be with you long.

Man and Wife

The month of May 2009,
Where all lovers dine,
Thirty days of my life,
We were common man,
And lovely wife.

How happy we were at the time,
Tasting fruitful wine,
Three weeks undisturbed,
Away from reality,
Perturbed.

The happiness now gone away,
Keeps our lust at bay,
All but a memory,
Keeps me lingering
Within fantasy.

The Taken

How coupled are we.
Spending an evening,
Just talking,
Relaxing.
Sharing painful memories
Of drunken fathers,
And scornful mothers.
A realization came.
A brick upon my soul.
How wrong I was,
A plan to hurt you,
When it's all too clear,
We're one in the same.
I can't be without you,
My ancient sweet guardian.
Familiar your bed is,
Soft are the sheets,
Cuddled with downy care
We lie as one.
Our shame pressing together
As fresh as the day
Adam and Eve cowered.

Hetairai

Walk in standing noble,
The pan is whispering,
In desperate,
Pleasant fleet.
Pregnant fruits are layered
To sacrifice.
Mashed in oils,
Goats cheese, and
Dried tomatoes,
A fetus covered
From a mothers exotic womb.
The Greek men feast,
On all that is woman.
Hetairai.
Flasks of the Pornai.
The flutist dies away,
When drunken harps,
All plucked with ease,
Coated with olive bind.
The tall,
The willing,
They take it all.
Enslaved, and dead
Inside.

Dreamers Legend

Utter bliss
Soaring through the fields,
He bends to kiss her,
Still he yields.

Cherries hang high,
In the gossamer trees,

Lying around the blossoms,
Touching
The falling leaves.

The smell of lilacs,
The grapes are all around,

Love within both
Are found.

Legend stays
Among the lovers

Beneath hot, sticky,
Honey covered covers.

Presence of a Goddess

Weeping inside, sitting,
You are on your knees,
Begging.
Cursing the treatment
Handed,
But throw away everything,
Seeing
A lovely face
Laughing.
Rosy cheeks
Blushing,
Your anger melts
Eternally,
But remains upon
Leaving.

She Is Mine

Alone I seethed. Aggravation.
Like bitter spoiled wine
I crushed the grapes alive,
Having seen the cellar
Cool and dry,
I came across a bottle;
Born in '89.

Accomplished then
And having known
Her flawless cry,
I would have set to grace,
And shook her father's hand
While auditing the family,
For which my soul had arrived.

Blindly wandering along,
The vintage before my eyes,
Nineteen years old
And broken from many lies,
I took her in my arms,
Tasting her succulent years,
I threw her in my bed,
And settled her burning rage.

Over time
I grew to love
Such splendid wine.

Upon every sitting
Those lips grew big
And sweeter,
Seducing my every limb
And eventually,
Conquering the impossible.

My heart.

Yet jealousy turned,
My darling precious
Was noticed by all,
And permanently divine
So anointed eternally,
Men bowed their heads
As thought she were
A new age Saint.

In this I fear
To lose her.
My soul altogether.

I am her greatest love,
She is my greatest half,
We are one,
Yet admittedly,
I roam selfishly,
Because I cannot provide,
What she needs inside.

Goodbye My King

Daubed in riches stolen,
Flaked in golden wealth,
Relaxed positioning,
In a tub of bloody health.

A trinket of desire,
Living through the night,
Myself watching others,
Implore the days delight.

Cannot move,
Cannot speak,
For the gods a fury,
Prophesize my future
Bleak.

I question all,
The dawn peaking,
Locks are put away,
And standing renewed,
Raped by the day,
An oil cone stands,
Oozing its victory,
Down a holy body.

I am reborn
A virgin once more,
And shut behind palace walls
Till the dusk needs its whore.

I am she no more.

Sacred teachings painted,
Chiseled on sanded walls,

For all that is remembered,
Were my triumphs
To the Pharaoh's beck and calls.

Like a needy child,
I coo on every sight,
For my King is the life,
Of all that is right.

So lasting securely,
Anubis takes his flight,
Packing the stolen gold,
Throwing the temptress delight,
And carries her away,
To all divinely sight.

Horus pecks away a tomb,
And carves her earthly name,
From petty value,
To eternal fame.

Path of Fixture

In the line of your eyes
I fall in disguise
To the shape
Of a polished reflection.
Modest, beautiful
Soft and pure,
All traits of which
You are certain, sure.
I dazzle,
As you say,
Having sprouted freckles
In a euphoric haze.
I glow,
And giggle,
In every gaze.

A Feast

Your soul to hold, how perfect and raw,
Through brown mirrors I feast,
Having left no morsel exposed,
I suck on your lips,
As thought they were eggs,
Filled with succulent chocolate cream.

Like a snake to its prey,
My body melts around you,
All becoming one in the ooze,
While we dive deep together,
Down to the core of passion.

I inhale the very breath, your last,
Locking your life, your secrets away,
And holding your hand,
Guiding you the way,
Eternally to perfection.

I weight your heart in time,
Squeezing its very core,
And keeping in rhythm,
Its count of beat.

The judgment of purity,
An honor to immortality,
The contract is named,

And the final walk through the gates,
Embraces all our memories.